POLAR BEARS

by Tamra B. Orr

Children's Press®

An Imprint of Scholastic Inc.
New York   Toronto   London   Auckland   Sydney
Mexico City   New Delhi   Hong Kong
Danbury, Connecticut

Content Consultant
Dr. Stephen S. Ditchkoff
Professor of Wildlife Sciences
Auburn University
Auburn, Alabama

Photographs © 2013: Alamy Images: 12 (Juan Gil), 35 (Steven J. Kazlowski); Arctic Photo/Bryan & Cherry Alexander: 39; Bob Italiano: 44 foreground, 45 foreground; Corbis Images/Sylvain Sonnet/Hemis: 31; Dreamstime: 5 bottom, 15 (Mirage3), 8 (Outdoorsman), 2 background, 3 background, 44 background, 45 background (Steve Allen); Getty Images/T. Davis/W. Bilenduke: cover; Media Bakery/Edward Bennett: 16; Shutterstock, Inc.: 28 (Eric Gevaert), 2 foreground, 3 foreground, 20 (FloridaStock), 5 top, 11 (Julie Simpson), 27 (Sergey Skleznev), 23 (Uryadnikov Sergey), 32 (zixian); Superstock, Inc.: 1, 4, 5 background, 7, 24, 46 (Animals Animals), 40 (Minden Pictures), 19 (NHPA), 36 (Wally Herbert/Robert Harding Picture Library Ltd.).

Library of Congress Cataloging-in-Publication Data
Orr, Tamra.
  Polar bears / by Tamra B. Orr.
      pages cm.—(Nature's children)
  Includes index.
  Audience: Ages 9–12.
  Audience: Grades 4–6.
  ISBN 978-0-531-20980-6 (lib. bdg.)
  ISBN 978-0-531-24306-0 (pbk.)
  1. Polar bear—Juvenile literature. I. Title.
  QL737.C27O77 2013
  599.786—dc23   2012034330

1 2 3 4 5 6 7 8 9 10 R 22 21 20 19 18 17 16 15 14 13

Polar Bears

Class	Mammalia
Order	Carnivora
Family	Ursidae
Genus	*Ursus*
Species	*Ursus maritimus*
World distribution	Throughout the Arctic
Habitat	Arctic sea ice, water, islands, and continental coastlines
Distinctive physical characteristics	Longer necks and heads than other bear species; coat varies in color from pure white to yellow; heavy, oily fur to protect against cold and moisture; males are two to three times as large as females
Habits	Solitary animals; mate in spring and have one to four cubs in the winter; spend as much time in the water as on land
Diet	Ringed and bearded seals, walruses, narwhals, beluga whales, and fish; is also known to eat birds' eggs, berries, and kelp on very rare occasions

POLAR BEARS

Contents

CHAPTER 1

Lords of the Arctic

A huge white bear lumbers across the ice deep in the Arctic. Two young cubs follow behind her. She stops when she comes across a hole in the ice. She crouches down beside it and waits, keeping watch quietly. Nearby, her cubs swipe at each other and wrestle playfully. Soon, they crouch down beside their mother. Everything is quiet.

Before long, a seal's nose bobs to the surface for a breath of air. Its head pops up. Suddenly, the mother polar bear swings her paw in a powerful blow, pulling the seal onto the ice. The polar bear and her cubs will have plenty to eat today!

Polar bears are **mammals**. They live near the **frigid** Arctic Ocean in places such as northern Russia, Alaska, Canada, Norway, and Denmark. They share their **habitat** with a few other **warm-blooded** animals, including caribou, arctic foxes, and snowy owls.

Polar bears are among the largest, most powerful mammals in the world.

A Foot-Long Paw

If you look at a picture of a polar bear surrounded by ice and snow, it may not look very big. But it is! Polar bears are actually the largest **carnivores** in the world.

An adult female polar bear weighs between 330 and 550 pounds (150 and 250 kilograms). Males are even bigger, sometimes weighing as much as 1,500 pounds (680 kg). That is as much as an entire classroom of 10-year-olds or a small car.

From one end to the other, these bears are also longer than most adult humans. They can reach lengths of around 8 feet (2.5 m). When polar bears stand up on their back legs, they are tall enough to look directly into a basketball hoop.

A close-up look at a polar bear's paw is enough to show anyone how truly huge these animals are. Each paw measures 12 inches (30.5 centimeters) across.

Adult Male
6 ft. (1.8 m)

Adult Male
Polar Bear
8 ft. long
(2.5 m)

Polar bears are very tall when they stand up on their hind legs.

Alone and at Rest

Searching for food and eating take up most of a polar bear's waking hours. An average polar bear must eat more than 4 pounds (2 kg) of fat or meat each day to avoid losing weight. On some days, a polar bear can find enough food without any trouble. On other days, it must go to sleep with a growling, empty stomach.

Polar bears spend a great deal of time resting or sleeping. When the weather is warmer, a polar bear goes to sleep to keep its body temperature low. A polar bear also sleeps whenever a storm arrives. It digs a small **den** in the snow and pushes its head inside the hole. Then it closes its eyes and waits for the storm to pass.

Polar bears spend most of their time alone. In the spring, mothers are often seen with their cubs. Adult pairs may be spotted together during **mating** season. The rest of the time, however, polar bears are **solitary**.

During some parts of the year, a polar bear might spend almost 90 percent of its time resting.

CHAPTER 2

Surviving in the Cold

Polar bears must cope with very cold temperatures all year long. Winters are freezing cold in the Arctic. Even the summers, which are short, are quite cool. The bears walk on snow and ice, and swim in freezing water. How do they manage to keep warm? The clues can be found in their fur and what lies underneath.

A polar bear's fur looks white, but it is not. It is made of hollow tubes that have little to no color of their own. The white snow and ice surrounding the bear make the fur look white. Under the fur is black skin. You can see this skin on the bear's nose. This dark skin holds the sun's heat and keeps the bear warmer.

The real key to a polar bear keeping warm lies beneath its skin, where there is a layer of fat that is 2 to 4 inches (5 to 10 cm) thick. This fat is called **blubber**. It holds heat in and makes it easier for the bear to float in the water.

Polar bears live in icy habitats that would be far too cold for most other animals.

Strong Swimmers

Much like walruses and seals, polar bears often spend as much time in the ocean as they do on land. It is not too surprising that its species name is *Ursus maritimus*, or "sea bear."

Polar bears are excellent swimmers. They can swim long distances without stopping. They swim in freezing cold water, but their fur keeps their bodies warm and dry. They swim as fast as 6 miles (9.6 kilometers) per hour, using their front feet to paddle and their back feet to steer. Polar bears can also hold their breath underwater for up to two minutes at a time.

In one experiment, scientists put tracking devices on more than 50 polar bears to see how far the animals could swim. They discovered that these strong bears can paddle hundreds of miles without stopping.

FUN FACT! In 2011, scientists observed a polar bear that swam nonstop for nine days.

Polar bears dive into freezing water in search of food.

d

...es a lot of hard work. Polar

...nting skills to get the right

...heir sharp teeth and claws, as well

...one of its greatest strengths. These bears

...se of smell. They can catch the scent of a

...n 0.5 miles (0.8 km) away. They can even smell

...et (0.9 m) under the snow. Polar bears can smell

...rom even farther away. Some experts call polar bears

...egs."

...r bear's 42 pointed teeth work like strong scissors when

... prey. Those teeth and the bear's extremely sharp claws

...to grab, hold, and tear apart a tasty animal.

UNFACT! Experts can determine a bear's age by slicing one of its teeth open and counting the rings inside.

Polar bears sniff at the air and the ground for clues that will lead them to their prey.

Ice Fishing

Polar bears are very patient hunters. They often use a method known as still hunting. A polar bear hunting this way sits quietly next to an airhole in the ice for most of the day. It waits and waits for a seal to come up into the hole to take a breath. When the seal finally appears, the bear grabs it and pulls it out onto the surface of the ice. Other times, the bear simply uses its paws to break the ice and then reaches into the water for a snack.

Polar bears sometimes hear seals moving around in their dens under the ice. The bear uses its strong paws to push on the ice until the roof of the seal's den caves in.

If there are not enough seals to catch, polar bears will make meals out of walruses, reindeer, or caribou. When these animals are hard to find, the bears will munch on foods such as berries, birds' eggs, or kelp.

Seals make up most of a polar bear's diet.

CHAPTER 3

Raising Babies at the North Pole

Polar bears, like many other animals, mate during spring. Each year in April and May, male polar bears begin searching for females who are ready to mate. They will travel great distances to find these females. Some have been observed tracking females as far as 62 miles (100 km).

There are usually more males who are ready to mate than there are females. As a result, male polar bears compete with each other for mates. Several males will follow a single female. One male will threaten another by lowering its head, opening its mouth, and roaring. If the other bear isn't frightened away, the two will fight. Polar bears rarely die during these fights, but they can suffer serious injuries. The winner continues pursuing the female, while the loser is chased away. Eventually, only the strongest male is left to mate with the female.

Polar bears sometimes stand up on their hind legs when they fight each other.

Digging a Den

After mating, a female polar bear's life gets very busy. With babies on the way, it is time for her to build a den. Most bears **hibernate**, but polar bears do not. The closest they get is when they dig a den to prepare for having babies. Polar bears usually dig their dens on hillsides or snowbanks. These dens are long and narrow. They measure around 5 feet (1.5 m) wide, 6.6 feet (2 m) long, and 3.3 feet (1 m) high. The insides of the dens are much warmer than the outside air.

Before going into the den to rest for several months, pregnant female bears eat as much as possible. They need to gain a lot of extra weight before their cubs are born. New mothers do not eat or drink for four to eight months after giving birth. They need the fat from their extra weight to **nurse** their babies.

Dens provide a hidden place for polar bear mothers to give birth and protect their newborn cubs.

Beautiful Baby Bears

Just six weeks after a polar bear enters her den, the big day arrives. It is time for the cubs to be born! **Litters** are usually made up of twins, but may have as few as one or as many as four cubs. Even though adult polar bears are huge animals, babies are only about the size of squirrels. They weigh less than 2 pounds (1 kg) each.

Newborn cubs have almost no hair or teeth. They cannot hear, see, or walk. They depend completely on their mother to survive. She keeps them warm and safe by cuddling and breathing on them.

The babies can see and hear once they are about a month old. After they grow to weigh about 20 pounds (9 kg), the polar bear cubs can come out of the den and start learning how to survive in their snowy habitat. This happens right around the time winter ends. At first, they stay near the den and continue to sleep there at night. Once the cubs get used to colder weather and build the muscles they need to walk longer distances, the mother begins leading them farther away from the den.

Cubs sometimes ride on their mother's back to travel through deep snow.

Learning Their Lessons

Male polar bears do not have anything to do with raising cubs. That responsibility belongs to the mother. Polar bear mothers are wonderful teachers. A female polar bear protects her cubs until they are two years old. During that time, she teaches them the skills they will need to stay safe and find food as adults.

A polar bear mother is sometimes so protective that she will stand up and roar at helicopters flying above her and her cubs. She keeps a close eye on her cubs because she knows they are at risk. Polar bear cubs often starve or are attacked by adult bears.

Cubs spend hours wrestling and tumbling as they grow up. All of this playing is fun, but it also teaches them how to fight for food and helps them build stronger muscles.

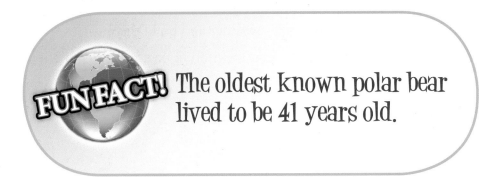

FUN FACT! The oldest known polar bear lived to be 41 years old.

Polar bear cubs wrestle and play, but do not hurt each other.

Out on Their Own

By the time they are two and a half or three years old, cubs have stopped nursing and have learned how to hunt and fight. They are grown. They no longer need their mother to help them find and kill enough food to eat. It is time for them to go live on their own.

It is up to the mother to let her cubs know when it is time to leave her side. Sometimes she simply wanders away. Other times, the cubs might not understand that their mother is trying to leave them. They keep following her wherever she goes. In these cases, the mother must chase her cubs away.

After leaving their mother, brothers and sisters often travel together for a few months. Over time, they split apart to go in different directions.

By the time a female polar bear turns four or five years old, she will give birth to her own cubs. Then the whole cycle begins again.

Until they are old enough to live on their own, polar bear cubs share a close relationship with their mother.

CHAPTER 4

Old Bears and New Bears

The types of bears that live today have only existed for around five million years. However, other types of bears were around long before modern species existed. The first bear species appeared sometime between 55 million and 38 million years ago. These ancient species are extinct now. However, they are the ancestors of the bear species that live today.

Studying ancient species can be very difficult. Because scientists do not have access to live animals, they must instead use fossils to learn about extinct species. By finding out how old a fossil is, they can figure out how long ago different species existed. Fossils can also help scientists learn how big extinct species were. For example, the largest known bear species in history is called the giant short-faced bear. These bears have been extinct for many years, but scientists know that some were 11 feet (3.4 m) long and weighed 2,000 pounds (907 kg). That is even bigger than a polar bear!

Fossils have helped scientists learn about ancient bears and other extinct animals.

Bears Big and Small

Today, there are eight different bear species living around the world. On average, the polar bear is the largest of them. However, the brown bear comes very close to matching its cousin. Though the average brown bear is smaller than the average polar bear, the largest known brown bear weighed almost 300 pounds (136 kg) more than the largest known polar bear. Brown bears live in mountains, meadows, and river valleys. They are sometimes called grizzly bears. Brown bears that live on Alaska's Kodiak Island are often called Kodiak bears.

The sun bear is the smallest bear species. Average males weigh about 100 pounds (45 kg). The largest polar bears weigh about fifteen times that much! Sun bears use their long tongues to lick honey out of beehives. Because of this, they are sometimes known as honey bears. They live in the forests of Southeast Asian countries such as Vietnam and Thailand. Sun bears have shorter, thicker fur than other bear species. This heavy fur keeps dirt and insects from reaching the bears' skin.

Brown bears have quick reflexes that enable them to snatch fish from the water.

A New Type of Bear

In the spring of 2006, a hunter shot a bear and noticed something very odd about it. It had white fur with brown patches. Testing showed the bear's mother was a polar bear, but the father was a grizzly. Experts were surprised by these findings. This type of **hybrid** had never been seen before. Another similar bear was found a few years later. This one had a hybrid mother and a grizzly father.

Scientists determined that in the spring, male grizzly bears sometimes leave their dens before the females do. As they wander around looking for mates, they may run into female polar bears that are searching for food.

No one is sure what to name these new bears. Some people call them "grolar bears," while others refer to them as "pizzly bears."

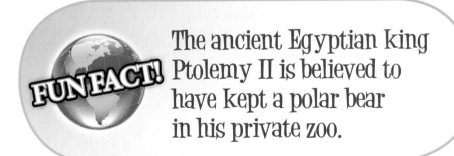

FUN FACT! The ancient Egyptian king Ptolemy II is believed to have kept a polar bear in his private zoo.

This hybrid polar bear shares the short neck and face coloring of a grizzly parent.

CHAPTER 5

Looking to the Future

There are fewer than 25,000 polar bears left on the planet. They are now considered **endangered**. This is a result of a combination of too much hunting and the effects of **global warming**.

Each year, hunters kill hundreds of polar bears. The Inuit respected the bears and only hunted what they needed to survive. However, most modern hunters kill polar bears for other reasons. Sport hunters pay thousands of dollars to go on polar bear hunts as an adventure. Other hunters kill the bears to sell their fur and body parts. Both of these types of hunting are a huge threat to the number of polar bears left in the world. Some countries have placed **bans** on hunting the bears. Others, such as Russia, limit how many can be killed each year.

Hunting is a major threat to polar bears in certain parts of the world.

A Warming Planet

Global warming is a threat that is hard to see and even harder to stop. Although the Arctic is very cold, it is not as cold as it used to be. The average temperature in the region has risen between 4 and 7 degrees Fahrenheit in the past 50 years. That may not sound like much, but a small increase can lead to big changes.

A higher temperature means that ice and snow melt earlier in the spring and freeze later in the winter. Polar bears depend on the sea ice for their hunting. If there is less ice, the bears are forced to swim farther to find food and a place to live. Less sea ice can also mean fewer seals. This raises the risk of starvation for polar bears.

Experts predict that the temperature in the Arctic will rise another 7 to 13 degrees Fahrenheit within the next century. If this happens, polar bears may go from endangered to extinct.

Melting ice could cause polar bear populations to shrink.

Scientific Studies

Many experts study polar bears to learn more about them and find new ways to help them. But how do you study an animal that is the size of a small car?

First, the bears are sedated. Scientists fly across the sea ice in a helicopter. They use dart guns to shoot polar bears from above. Drugs in the darts can knock a bear out cold. Then the bear is either measured right where it falls or taken to a research center for further testing.

Scientists often take blood samples from the bears. They also attach ear tags so they can track the animals' movements. A few bears are given special radio collars. These collars send signals to satellites. This allows scientists to chart the bears' movements on a computer. Anything they can learn to help the polar bear survive longer is a victory!

Scientists must make sure polar bears are unconscious before taking measurements or blood samples.

Words to Know

ancestors (AN-ses-turz) — ancient animal species that are related to modern species

bans (BANZ) — rules that forbid people from doing something

blubber (BLUHB-ur) — the layer of fat under the skin of a large marine animal

carnivores (KAR-nih-vorz) — animals that have meat as a regular part of their diet

den (DEN) —the home of a wild animal

endangered (en-DAYN-jurd) — at risk of becoming extinct, usually because of human activity

extinct (ik-STINGKT) — no longer found alive

fossils (FOSS-uhlz) — the hardened remains of prehistoric plants and animals

frigid (FRIJ-id) — extremely cold in temperature

global warming (GLOH-buhl WORM-ing) — a gradual rise in the temperature of Earth's atmosphere, caused by human activities that pollute

habitat (HAB-uh-tat) — the place where an animal or a plant is usually found

hibernate (HYE-bur-nayt) — to sleep through the winter in order to survive when temperatures are cold and food is hard to find

hybrid (HYE-brid) — a plant or animal that has parents of two different types or species

kelp (KELP) — a large, edible, brown seaweed

litters (LIT-urz) — numbers of baby animals that are born at the same time to the same mother

mammals (MAM-uhlz) — warm-blooded animals that have hair or fur and usually give birth to live young

mating (MAYT-ing) — joining together to produce babies

nurse (NURS) — to feed a baby milk from a breast

prey (PRAY) — an animal that's hunted by another animal for food

satellites (SAT-uh-lites) — spacecraft that are sent into orbit around Earth, the moon, or another heavenly body

sedated (suh-DAY-tid) — put to sleep using drugs

solitary (SOL-ih-tehr-ee) — preferring to live alone

warm-blooded (WORM-BLUHD-id) — describing animals whose body temperature stays about the same, even if the temperature around them is very hot or very cold

Habitat Map

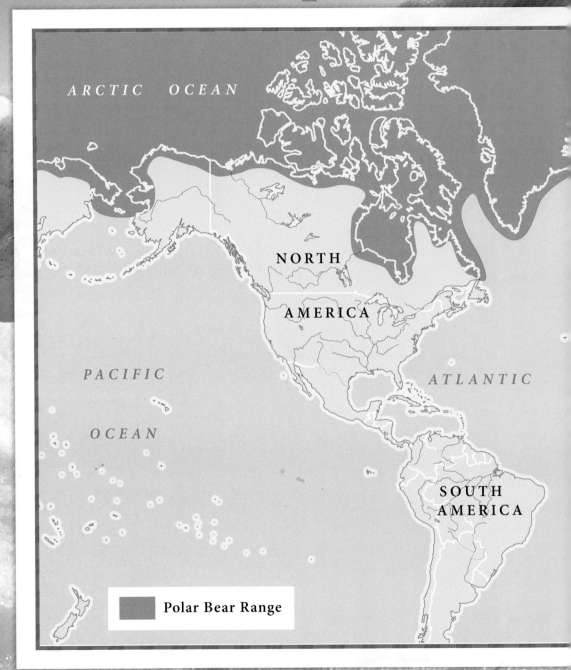

ARCTIC OCEAN

NORTH
AMERICA

PACIFIC

OCEAN

ATLANTIC

SOUTH
AMERICA

Polar Bear Range

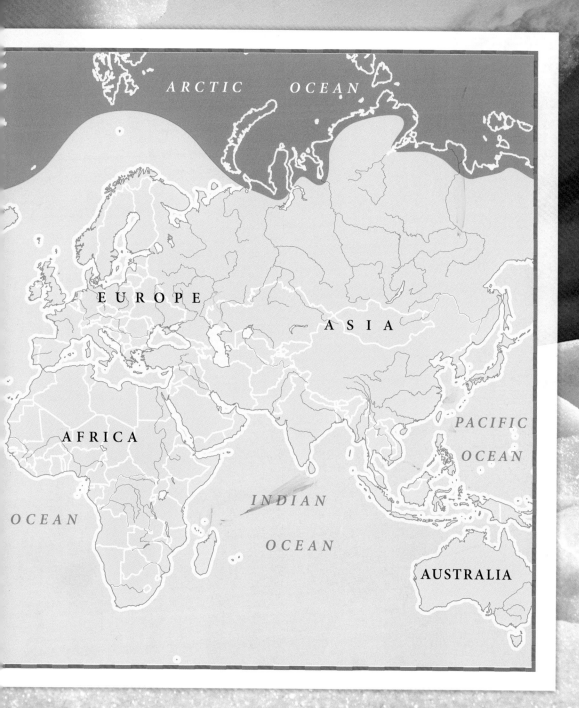

ARCTIC OCEAN

EUROPE

ASIA

AFRICA

PACIFIC
OCEAN

OCEAN

INDIAN

OCEAN

AUSTRALIA

Find Out More

Books

Hirsch, Rebecca E. *Top 50 Reasons to Care About Polar Bears: Animals in Peril.* Berkeley Heights, NJ: Enslow Publishers, 2010.

Lourie, Peter. *The Polar Bear Scientists.* Boston: Houghton Mifflin Books for Children, 2012.

Rosing, Norbert and Elizabeth Carney. *Face to Face with Polar Bears.* Washington D.C.: National Geographic, 2007.

Visit this Scholastic Web site for more information on polar bears:
www.factsfornow.scholastic.com
Enter the keywords **Polar Bears**

Index

Page numbers in *italics* indicate a photograph or map.

About the Author

Tamra B. Orr is the author of more than 300 nonfiction books for all ages. She is a graduate of Ball State University and currently lives in the Pacific Northwest with her husband, children, cat, and dog. Orr has written about many different parts of the world and the amazing creatures found throughout it, but polar bears remain one of her favorites.